Heal

Inspire

Love

"Affirmations for the soul"

By

Moonsoulchild & Michael Tavon

Other Works by Moonsoulchild

Journey Through My Heart Vol. 1 & 2
I Was Never Broken
Letters to You
Dear Anonymous
Young Naked Soul
The Feelings and Healing Collection

Other Works by Michael Tavon

Nirvana: Pieces of Self-Healing vol 1& 2
A Day Without Sun
Songs for Each Mood
Young Heart, Old Soul
Don't Wait Til I Die to Love Me
Dreaming in a Perfect World

3 | h e a l   i n s p i r e   l o v e

You've failed at love so many times you've convinced yourself it's an impossible feat. Take this into consideration; If someone failed to love you, it's not a failure; it's a lesson and a blessing. They gave you the space to find true happiness when they disappointed you.

-    Michael Tavon

Treat your mind like the beautiful plant it is by watering it with positive thoughts. Self-doubt is the poison that will hinder its growth. Let go of toxic doubts to grow inward.

- Michael Tavon

Find the type of love that makes heartache irrelevant. The type of love that never reminds you of pain. The kind of love that inspires you to overcome your fears. The kind of love brings your heart comfort.

-    Michael Tavon

Self-doubt will be the tallest wall your mind
will build, but as all long as you climb,
Gradually, each day, you will find yourself on
the other side, eventually.

-      Michael Tavon

See the light in being alone.
Praise your solitude.
You will learn so much about you just by
spending quality time by yourself.

-    Michael Tavon

To make strides to success, the first thing you must do is adapt a positive language. Change "I can't" to "I'll find a way. Change "I'm not like" to "there's no one like me.

-   Michael Tavon

Toxic people will remind you of your past mistakes when you're outgrowing yourself as well as them. Your mistakes are part of your growth and shall never be held against you when you're bettering yourself.

-   Michael Tavon

If you genuinely wish to grow mentally, read something that offers a fresh, challenging perspective. Reading material solely because it's relatable to you will make you feel good, but you won't gain much from it.

-    Michael Tavon

Never be embarrassed to ask questions;
there's no shame in not knowing. There's no
shame in acquiring knowledge.

-     Michael Tavon

You don't owe anyone an explanation on,
how you dream, how you love and
what you believe.

The things that keep your heart racing
are not open for debate or interpretation.
Never allow anyone to water your passions
with doubt.

-    Michael Tavon

Have more faith in yourself and believe in your instincts. When you constantly second guess yourself, you will only make your path more complicated than it has to be.

-    Michael Tavon

It's time to release the grudges holding you back; they're not helping you move forward. What's done is done; holding grudges will not resolve anything. Life is too short to hold onto the past.

-   Michael Tavon

Protect your dreams with a bulletproof vest, so when people try to shoot you down, the bullets will fail to penetrate.

-    Michael Tavon

Remain inspired by others but never compare yourself. There's nothing wrong with being competitive, but when you compare someone else's success to where you are now, you will lose confidence. Study your field, become a student. Never do it for clout or money; you'll always be running behind others doing that. Do it for love.

-    Michael Tavon

Say this aloud:

I will no longer let regret consume me.

I will no longer allow pain to control me.

I will no longer let fear make my decisions.

I will move on.

I will become stronger.

I live fearlessly.

- Michael Tavon

You cannot carry someone's burdens while trying to balance your own.

-    Michael Tavon

Instead of belittling yourself because of your
flaws, compliment yourself more often.

-      Michael Tavon

Write 10 things you love about yourself below:

1.

2.

3.

4.

5.

6.

7.

8.

9.

10.

Love is not a battle, whoever taught you this fooled you. A real mature love will challenge you in every right way possible.

-    Michael Tavon

Self-doubt cripples the mind that aspires to fly.

-     Michael Tavon

Happiness, like any emotion, is fleeting, so it shouldn't be the goal. You'll find yourself endlessly chasing the impossible. You should focus on making peace with your pain and understanding the why. Once you find the clarity you deserve, your wings will finally spread.

-    Michael Tavon

Your passion may rub others the wrong way,
your drive will make others jealous. Your
dreams will make you misunderstood by your
loved ones. This only means you're not an
average person. This confirms that you're on
the right path.

- Michael Tavon

It's perfectly natural to feel nervous when the universe presents an opportunity that will change your life. It's okay, but never allow that voice in your head to convince you that you're not worthy of this moment. You've worked your ass off to get here; you deserve it. Breath and be fearless; your time is now.

-     Michael Tavon

Be mindful of what you give your energy to.
Every action does not deserve a reaction. Not
every negative remark deserves a response.
Once you realize a lot of your stress comes
from reacting to things that do not deserve
your time, you will find it easier to block
negativity.

-    Michael Tavon

Promise not to give up when you fall short.
Promise not to lose sight when the path
becomes unclear. Promise you will grow from
every mistake. Promise that the passion
burning inside of you never dies.

-     Michael Tavon

Words to say when you feel broken:

No one can make me feel powerless; my love
is infinite, and no matter how many times
people try to drain my heart, I will always have
the strength to love harder than ever before.

-     Michael Tavon

The road to self-healing does not have shortcuts and features many speed humps and potholes. You may have to reroute or take a few U-turns; it's all part of the journey; no one said it would be a smooth ride. Never allow the mishaps to discourage your progress. Always move forward.

-    Michael Tavon

Note to old lovers,

I don't need you checking up on me. I don't need you to pretend you care. I don't want to revisit old memories or catch up with you. If you must know, life has been amazing since you lost me. You've helped me move onto more incredible things, and I thank you for that.

-    Michael Tavon

The perfect love will always be there, waiting for you. There's no need to force anything. There's no need to rush. Continue to grow into your own. Love will find you once you discover yourself.

-    Michael Tavon

You gotta learn to see people for who they are, not for who you want them to be.

-    Michael Tavon

Learn the difference between having goals
and putting unnecessary pressure on yourself;
sometimes you're not ready, don't beat
yourself up when you fall short.

-       Michael Tavon

If you're an artist, practice your craft like it's a religion. YOU WILL NEVER BECOME PERFECT at what you do, so do not stress over that.

-    Michael Tavon

If you're unable to do something on your own, it's okay to ask for help; there's no shame in that.

-      Michael Tavon

Stop overthinking. You can't control
everything. Sometimes you just gotta do it.

-     Michael Tavon

Do not regret old versions of yourself; without them, you will not be who you are today.

- Michael Tavon

Your mind has a way of convincing you to believe whatever it wants you to believe; make sure you tell yourself how amazing you are each day; eventually, you will believe that too.

- Michael Tavon

Love is so synonymous with pain because humans have been doing it wrong since the beginning of time.

-    Michael Tavon

When you're torn between giving up and
moving forward, take the ladder, always.

-    Michael Tavon

Be so confident it makes the older versions of you proud.

-    Michael Tavon

Change your perception. There's a lesson to be learned in everything. As we grow, as we age, obstacles like heartache, rejections, and setbacks, will continue to push us over the edge, but the goal is to push through to become stronger, wiser, and more loving.

- Michael Tavon

Your day job does not define you. Never allow anyone to shame you for holding a steady job to meet ends while you're investing in your dreams. Simple-minded people won't understand this. Keep working; God got you.

-    Michael Tavon

Stop seeking validation from people outside of yourself. Brag about yourself publicly without coming off as arrogant. You deserve the praise. Clap for everything you've accomplished.

-    Michael Tavon

Instead of calling it heartbreak
Call it a fresh start
Instead of calling it a 'mistake'
Call it a lesson
Instead of calling it rejection
Call it "Room for Improvement"

Condition your mind to believe that life's
shortcomings are opportunities for growth.

-      Michael Tavon

Boundaries are essential for your mental health. Don't bend or break them to make everyone feel comfortable. Never allow anyone to cross those boundaries for the sake of love or friendships.

-    Michael Tavon

Healing may seem impossible when reminders of the past keep flashing before your eyes. Before you give up, think about how far you've come. Your worst days are behind, and your best days are waiting to be claimed.

-    Michael Tavon

You're never lost when soul searching.

-     Michael Tavon

Just because you've found yourself at a dead-end, it doesn't mean there isn't a better route for you to take. There are many roads to success. Keep on, keeping on.

-   Michael Tavon

Sometimes it's best to step back, take a break from people and responsibilities. Your body deserves it; your mind needs it. Never feel guilty for recharging your spirit.

-    Michael Tavon

True bliss lives far away from your comfort
zone.

-    Michael Tavon

Once I finally let go of the past. Time went by at a slower pace. I became more settled and less anxious. I learned how to enjoy the moment I became infatuated with my present self.

-     Michael Tavon

You're young and trying to find your way to
continue to acquire knowledge and explore
new interests. You don't have to settle for
what's familiar because you fear how others
may perceive you.

-       Michael Tavon

Stop settling for bums because you hate being alone. You can't motivate a bum to change. They will only use and manipulate you with empty promises. You'll find yourself chasing after potential that's not there.

- Michael Tavon

When your lover says you've improved their quality of life, it's truly the most profound compliment. Introducing methods that improve your lover's physical, mental, and spiritual being creates an infinite type of love, an unbreakable bond.

-      Michael Tavon

You're still a growth in progress. You're still learning how to process your emotions before expressing yourself verbally.

- Michael Tavon

Note to self:

The voice of doubt saying you aren't good enough is just an illusion you have created. You're afraid of what the future may hold. Stop doubting yourself; you're working too damn hard to quit. You deserve every blessing coming to you.

-   Michael Tavon

You've come too far to give up now. You've come too far to throw away your hard work. You've come too far to allow self-doubt to win. You've come too far, way too far. Be proud of yourself. You deserve it all.

-      Michael Tavon

Look at you, accomplishing things! Getting your life in order and minding yo business. Living yo best life with as little drama as possible. Even while going through some shit, you handle it with grace. You deserve everything that's coming.

-    Michael Tavon

Bask in the ambiance of your individuality, you
were created to shed the unique light you
were given. You're only dimming your shine
by chasing stars that were not meant for you.

-      Michael Tavon

You got away, you're connecting with yourself again, even if it means picking up the pieces. Don't give up on yourself, or the love you'll find in yourself and share with someone who treats you how you deserve.
Don't let a toxic person change you.

-   Moonsoulchild

Don't let someone's insecurities dim your own light. Their insecurities aren't your fault, don't make them your problem. It's an endless war trying to save someone from themselves; you'll never win because the problem was never within you, only within them.

- Moonsoulchild

I pray you wake up and see the beauty you've been leaving behind because you don't see yourself as beautiful. I pray you stop giving your heart to some, so quickly, who just take advantage. I pray you find yourself through the pain and your strength. Don't let today pass you by.

-    Moonsoulchild

We all were born to stand out. We all were made to be beautiful; it just takes years to acknowledge we don't need to *fit in* that our beauty comes from within.

- Moonsoulchild

Self-love is hard to discover. You may search for years to uncover that love. If only it was as easy as giving your heart to the ones who didn't deserve it.

-    Moonsoulchild

Self-love is the most challenging chapter in your life to uncover. There are so many dimensions to loving every part of you. Accepting your flaws and how they tie into your beauty. Letting go of old habits that created toxic behavior, bringing in the new, the growth, and lastly, the love.

-       Moonsoulchild

Sometimes we're afraid to move on because we hold faith close to our hearts hoping that people change. Sometimes we're in love with the idea of love, and we attach it to anyone who gives us an ounce.

- Moonsoulchild

You're as beautiful as the sun during the day and as comforting as the moon at night. *Your beauty will always shine brighter than the stars.*

-    Moonsoulchild

We need to teach less self-destruction and more self-love. We need to stop giving ourselves so easily to people with hearts that don't match ours or aren't meant to fit. We need to stop chasing. We need to stop trying to fill a void that can only be discovered within.

-   Moonsoulchild

Don't be afraid to go ghost when you feel it's time to close the door; some people outlived their entitlement to an explanation.
Sometimes you did all you could, said what you felt and still wasn't heard. Sometimes silence is the explanation.
Sometimes silence brings us peace.

-    Moonsoulchild

A **soulmate** isn't everyone you love throughout your life. A **soulmate** is someone who walks into your life and teaches you a love you never felt. It's a connection your heart can't deny. An unbreakable force. Not just a lover, a soulmate comes in all forms; cherish them all.

-    Moonsoulchild

Don't forget to choose yourself when it comes to almost losing yourself. Don't let it come to the point you need to dig yourself out of the same hole you let yourself fall into.

- Moonsoulchild

Don't let old pain, old friends, old flames cloud your judgment and make you believe it was your fault why you're no longer apart of their life. They didn't see the real in you; their heart wasn't as they made it seem, and that's not your fault.

-       Moonsoulchild

Love someone who doesn't place you into barriers, not someone who has you falling into habits which question your mental health. No one who loves you will bring you down a dark path. It just so happens they don't love themselves, which results in them loving you in the dark.

-    Moonsoulchild

Stop making excuses for how they love you when you know they don't. If they did, they wouldn't treat you like you're easy to lose. They know to you, they're irreplaceable. Find your voice, stop making excuses for people who only use you for their needs.

-    Moonsoulchild

You're not for everyone; the way you love
may scare some away, with a heart of love
that runs deep and unconditional. It's
important to know, it's not about the way you
love, but maybe they're not ready to love
someone like you.

-    Moonsoulchild

Someone out there is ready to love you, so don't give your energy to the ones who aren't. Even if love was once felt on both sides, when one disconnects, let love be lost and move on, but hold that love in your heart forever.

-    Moonsoulchild

Free yourself from the burdens you've been hoarding from old demons. Set yourself free from the bridges you burnt. Set yourself free from poisoned souls who only meant to intoxicate you. Set fire to your past, and watch the light lead you to your new path.

-      Moonsoulchild

It's true, people can change, but it's only possible if they want to. Timing plays a role in every connection you make, you can pick up where you left off years later, or you can completely forget where you left off. It's already written, don't question it.

-      Moonsoulchild

It's important to stay strong through the parts of life that challenge you, the parts you're searching for you.

-    Moonsoulchild

Let people be themselves without trying to
understand why.

-      Moonsoulchild

Love isn't painful.
Love isn't a constant force.
Love is a feeling that can't be denied,
only some lie.

-      Moonsoulchild

Always go to bed happy.
Never go to bed regretting your day,
regardless of how it ends; always be thankful
that you saw another day. Pray for your
blessings; pray you'll see better days. Always
be grateful to live the life you do; some aren't
so lucky.

Nothing bad stays, remember that.

-    Moonsoulchild

Find your worth and keep it safe; many people won't even try but will have you lose yourself while loving them.

-    Moonsoulchild

Treat your being with the same love; you
always give to everyone you hold close.

-      Moonsoulchild

Healing from the unknown could be scary because we convince ourselves closure within the other person is crucial, but forget, if you find peace and can move forward, that's the only closure you need.

-    Moonsoulchild

If something you wanted but resisted at first,
it's a sign that it's not meant for you. What's
not meant for you will always find a way to
pass you. What's right will never make you
think twice.

-    Moonsoulchild

You glow different when you're happy, so find
that glow. Find your happiness and let go
what's holding you back from it.

-       Moonsoulchild

Never forget to tell the ones you love that you love them. No grudges. Don't leave things on bad terms. Life's too short.

- Moonsoulchild

Don't be afraid to explore the connections you have with people. Don't be afraid to love who the universe presents to your life at the exact moment they walk in. I believe we have many soulmates. Don't overlook anyone who presents a soul connection; your heart will know.

-    Moonsoulchild

What hurts the heart most isn't all the love it gave, but the rejection of not feeling like our love was enough.

-    Moonsoulchild

Stop the habit of overlooking when people hurt you. Whether it's a family member, friend, or lover. If they become toxic to your being, they shouldn't be kept. Love them from afar. Go ghost. Don't ever feel ashamed for choosing your sanity over hurting them.

-      Moonsoulchild

Don't spend too much time on something you know may never last, but don't give up on something if you feel in your heart it's real. Accept the fact people change, things change, and nothing stays the same.
Sometimes you need to just let go.

-   Moonsoulchild

Just because you're born to love doesn't mean everyone is someone to love. Just because you have a connection doesn't mean you're soulmates. Just because you gave all you had, and it didn't get it reciprocated, doesn't mean give up. Love will find you when it's time.

-       Moonsoulchild

There's negativity everywhere.
You won't win if you react to everyone who
throws a curve ball your way. To win is to not
react. Block anything that isn't bringing you
blessings.

-     Moonsoulchild

I pray you find the light that's been hiding behind the darkness. I pray you realize there's no love in what's forced or not reciprocated. I pray you stop chasing someone you thought you loved. I pray you find the light that makes sense of everything you thought you knew.

- Moonsoulchild

You outgrow people you once loved; once you outgrow the old version of you they loved. We get lost "outgrowing" because we forget there's room for growth and often confuse growth with change. If they're not growing with you, you'll outgrow them, and it's okay.

- Moonsoulchild

If anyone ever makes you choose, choose you over them. Save you because saving them will only become a war you'll never win.

-    Moonsoulchild

Fill your life with people who only want to see you do better than them because that's what love is, you know you'll never be better because there's no competition. Anyone who wants less for you isn't the best for you.

-      Moonsoulchild

Do your best to love yourself without hitting roadblocks that lead you nowhere. Stop loving people who only make it hard. Love yourself today, and tomorrow, and forever. Promise me you'll try, and I'll promise you, you'll fall in love with you.

-    Moonsoulchild

You live to take chances, don't live to worry about the outcome. You could miss the moment of your life that could create your whole future, fearing what could go wrong. Live a little, live on the edge, and love with your whole heart. I promise nothing could ever break you.

-    Moonsoulchild

I promise you'll meet someone who will find the beauty within your flaws. I promise you'll find the beauty not only within your flaws but within your scars. Your past is just a reflection of the person you used to be, not the person you're growing to become.

-       Moonsoulchild

Let the opinions and all the assumptions on who you should be, who they think you are, go. Stop letting them tell you who you are when you know who you are and how much you love you. If they can't love you, they shouldn't. Stop listening to the noise.

-      Moonsoulchild

Your soul is beautiful. Your heart is just as beautiful, Don't ever forget that, even though you may get lost within the hurt, you're always going to remain true. Don't let the pain define you into something you're not.

-    Moonsoulchild

When the first thing you do, is wake up and there's chaos, turn to positive reminders: *there's so much more left of the day to make great.* Sometimes life comes to test you, and you need to remind it: **you're not going to get disappointed over every little thing**.

-    Moonsoulchild

Sometimes it's about forgiving when it wasn't your fault. It's making peace for your sake because your sanity is more important.

-   Moonsoulchild

Some will use your mental illness as a weapon, not understanding how weak it makes you. Some will bully you until you've hit your breaking point, then pray for you when you've hit rock bottom. It's hard being strong in a world with people trying to turn you against yourself.

- Moonsoulchild

I pray you all find someone
who matches your soul
the exact amount needed,
to fulfill that missing piece.
But before you find them,
I pray you find you.

-     Moonsoulchild

Don't ever second guess giving a compliment.
If you're thinking it, express it, you never
know if they might need it. You could change
their whole day.

- Moonsoulchild

Don't give up when times get rough and the days are looking dark. Don't give up when you fall short of a goal you should of accomplished months or years; there's always more time. Just don't give up.

-    Moonsoulchild

Even as a work in progress, you should always think of yourself as the best version of yourself. Look at what you've become, how far you've gotten, always be proud of your growth, and stop beating yourself up because you're not yet where you want to be.

-       Moonsoulchild

The insecurities you're facing are past mistakes coming to haunt you. They were created by not feeling good enough because you were made to feel like you weren't. It comes back to once upon a time, but today, overcome those insecurities like you overcame how they were created.

-     Moonsoulchild

I pray you rest well tonight. I pray all your worries, troubles, and fears don't keep you awake tonight. I pray for whatever it is keeping you from resting passes soon to place you at peace. I'm praying for you.

-     Moonsoulchild

Not every relationship can be "fixed" don't let anyone make you feel like you're wrong for walking away, instead of trying to save the love that's no longer love when it's become toxic. Some things aren't meant to be recovered.

-    Moonsoulchild

You're deserving of the same love you give.
You're beautiful even if you don't see it.
Sometimes you forget who you are, but it's
time to remind yourself how amazing you are
and take over the world today.

-    Moonsoulchild

It's essential to be with someone who brings peace to the darkness of your mind when you need balance you can't provide for yourself. You can be at peace with yourself, but when the one you love can keep you at peace, it's unmatchable.

-    Moonsoulchild

If someone doesn't take care of your soul the
way it should be handled, walk away; life's too
short to keep letting them damage you while
draining you of all the good you have left.
Life's too short to hold onto people who've
already let go.

-     Moonsoulchild

Some people are so ego-driven it's hard for
them to see the real in you because they're
worried about the last person who hurt them,
they put the past onto you and expect you to
fix them, and when you don't, their burdens
become your hurt too—don't let a toxic
person consume you.

-    Moonsoulchild

Don't settle; it's essential to ALWAYS give
your soul exactly what it needs to fulfill what
it needs, to complete you. Remember, just
because you "love" something or someone
doesn't mean you will forever. Sometimes
there's pain, you part ways, or you grieve the
loss.

-      Moonsoulchild

Practice self-love by taking care of yourself
before taking care of anyone who drives you
to believe their care is more important than
your sanity.

\-   Moonsoulchild

Sometimes it's best to let go when you can still hold the good of someone without creating too much pain, so in memory, you always remember the times they brought the most to your life—those are the most critical times.

-    Moonsoulchild

Don't wait until someone's life is over to support them. You'll end up feeling guilty whether you were there enough or could have done more—while latching to anything that contains memory. Support people you love; let them know they're loved while alive when it's most important.

-    Moonsoulchild

Being afraid to take chances will always keep you unhappy. Don't think twice if it's something that could change your life for the better.

- Moonsoulchild

I hope you always choose yourself if you're ever faced with that decision. I hope you always remember how important you are.

-       Moonsoulchild

Don't let anyone make you feel you're not worthy because you have the biggest heart; some may never understand because some may never be ready for it.

-       Moonsoulchild

I hope you wake up today thankful for seeing another day. I hope you wake up today and realize that sometimes things don't work out as planned—but that doesn't mean you give up. Pray for the things you want to happen, and watch them blossom.

-     Moonsoulchild

Love is beautiful; anyone who tells you otherwise hasn't experienced the love that awakens the soul and opens the heart. The kind of love you don't have to chase, try, or prove. The kind of love that's not only felt by you but within them too. The kind of love that inspires you.

-       Moonsoulchild

I promise you, if you let go of everything that is holding you back from true happiness, you will find it. You waste so much time trying to help others figure themselves out while they're draining you. It sounds selfish, but their problems aren't your problems. Take care of yourself.

-    Moonsoulchild

It's a goal to be with someone for the rest of your life. But make sure you're happy, secure, and loved unconditionally. Don't settle because you think it's too late; love has no timing, your soulmate is out there and waiting to love you.

-    Moonsoulchild

Not everyone is someone who's meant to stay; when the bad takes itself out of the story, stop blaming yourself.

-        Moonsoulchild

We need to learn, just because someone hurt us, shame on them, but when we become aware and we let them continue, it's shame on us.

-      Moonsoulchild

The love will always stay within your heart, but their presence won't be the same; sometimes you need to love from afar. It's okay to walk away without looking back or explaining why. Some people don't deserve an explanation on why they keep damaging your heart. Choose yourself.

-    Moonsoulchild

Don't forget to use your voice when it comes to anyone trying to take advantage of your heart.

-    Moonsoulchild

Being selfish isn't bad if you're doing what's best for you. At the end of the day, you're the only person who will have you when the rest walk away.

-   Moonsoulchild

Being family doesn't mean you should allow toxicity. It doesn't give them a pass—it doesn't make them good people. You're not obligated to love your family just because you think you have to. I have friends who are more like family. Love who shows you they do too. Let go of who hurts you.

-    Moonsoulchild

Find closure within the parts of your past you're still holding close to your heart. You've let go of the toxicity that's holding you back from happiness. Stop letting the memories of the bad consume you from being free.

-    Moonsoulchild

Stop letting the same people get to you in ways only you should control. Don't let them ruin your day off outcomes you've created, knowing they'll never match your energy. Put effort into finding your happiness, don't make them a priority when you're an option.

-     Moonsoulchild

Take a moment to remember the good times that have happened this year and compare them with the bad times. You'll learn that bad times don't last; something better always appears. Use those bad times as an example of why you should never give up.

-   Moonsoulchild

Do not let the ones who can't see your worth anywhere near your heart. They don't deserve to have an opinion on who you are now; they can only judge who you use to be. Your growth is new to them, don't let them get to you; you're doing great without them.

-    Moonsoulchild

Focus on TODAY. Don't focus on fixing yesterday's wrongs, don't focus on what tomorrow might bring. Life's too difficult to understand sometimes, and it's also too short to analyze.

-     Moonsoulchild

Free yourself from the burdens you've been hoarding from old demons. Set yourself free from the bridges you burnt—set yourself free from poisoned souls who only meant to intoxicate you. Set fire to your past, and watch the light lead you to your new path.

-    Moonsoulchild

Stop holding ties to worthless people—you're
holding onto people who only make you
believe your wrong when you've done nothing
but love these people in hopes they'll love you
the same in return. Let the burdens of them
free, as you will then be free of them.

-       Moonsoulchild

Take a break from giving your all to everyone, and take a moment to care for your heart, mind, and temple. You don't need to always be there for everyone; you're only human. If they can't understand you deserve a day alone, that should show their place in your life.

-   Moonsoulchild

Anyone who drains you of all your love and makes you take from you to give to them doesn't deserve any part of you.

- Moonsoulchild

Never run from the signs when you know you saw them, accept people disappear from your life only for a blessing to appear. Let go of what's gone. Never change your heart because you lessen your worth for someone who doesn't know theirs.

-      Moonsoulchild

Don't be afraid to be vulnerable. It's important to feel every emotion. Stop mistreating your heart because you've given too much and always loved too much. Those are beautiful traits, it just so happens, not everyone deserves them. Don't give up; someone will feel it, I promise.

-    Moonsoulchild

I pray today brings you the strength to see the real in people you love, that only bring you pain. I pray you find a way to make peace with the fact they no longer fit with you, and I pray you never let someone give you less than you deserve, ever again in this lifetime.

-   Moonsoulchild

Every day is a new opportunity to start where you left off. Every day is a new day to start over. Every day is another day. Today, be thankful you get a chance to make things right or start completely over and find your happiness, don't give up.

- Moonsoulchild

I hope you smile a little more today, and I hope you don't let anything or anyone take away your happiness. Little things are like roadblocks, don't let them interfere with your vision of your happiness. You're glowing.

-    Moonsoulchild

As lost as you feel now, you'll realize through this whole process, you always knew who you are—you were just comfortable—like a moon in the night sky, beautiful yet unreadable, there's nothing wrong with being a mystery to the world—as long as you never lose yourself.

-    Moonsoulchild

There's no map to discovering your true self.
You just need to open your eyes and heart, be
aware of the things you love, the people you
love, and how every piece ties into who you
are.

- Moonsoulchild

I promise you'll fail at love every time if you continue to only love when you're lonely.

-    Moonsoulchild

Leave who drowns your soul in sadness, hatred—in the dark. Don't let people who can't love themselves let you forget who you are. The way you wear your heart on your sleeve is beautiful, but I promise falling in love with yourself is even more beautiful.

-    Moonsoulchild

I know how hard it can be to set yourself free of toxic energy. But I promise, once you do, it's like a breath of fresh air. Putting your energy where it's only reciprocated will have you on cloud nine. Which results in the best decision you can make.

-   Moonsoulchild

I assure you, the more you keep up with someone else's life, the more miserable you'll become trying to compete where you don't belong. Not everyone's meant to go down the same road—stop following them, start creating your own path.

-    Moonsoulchild

Stop letting the same people get to you in ways only you should control. Don't let them ruin your day off outcomes you've created, knowing they'll never match your energy. Put effort into finding your happiness, don't make them a priority when you're an option.

-   Moonsoulchild

If someone continues to hurt you, you should think hard if holding onto them is what's best. Love isn't strong enough to hold together what's outgrown. Love is only strong when it's reciprocated; if it's not, you're fighting a battle you'll never win.

- Moonsoulchild

After trying to make someone understand
love and loyalty, you'll realize you shouldn't
have to prove your love when actions showed
up more times than you can count. When
loyalty never vanished.

-       Moonsoulchild

If you feel you gave all you could, if you feel you're now taking away from you, walk away, and I mean that without hesitation. They don't care enough to change their toxic ways after admitting to those traits, don't care enough to keep holding onto them.

-    Moonsoulchild

If you find peace in their absence, it's probably best to not hold onto them any longer.

-    Moonsoulchild

You'll never be truly happy if you're in everyone's lane but your own.

-       Moonsoulchild

I may not know your struggles or your everyday life, but I do know nothing is worth taking your own life. Your life matters. You matter. Every day we're thrown something we might not know how to handle, but it's not the end. You always have the chance to make good out of the bad.

-    Moonsoulchild

When you fall in love with someone who reciprocates the same love—someone who takes the time to actually understand your soul and loves you unconditionally, that's beautiful. I pray everyone feels this and not the love everyone believes to be painful.

-       Moonsoulchild

Be thankful for another day. Be thankful no matter how the day starts or ends, some weren't as lucky—don't take your life for granted, appreciate it regardless of the good or the bad, and I promise, many blessings will come your way.

-   Moonsoulchild

Daily Reminders:

Do something you love today.

Love yourself today.

Set one goal for today.

Take care of your mental health.

Tell someone you love, you love them.

Instagram:

@moonsoulchild

@bymichaeltavon

Twitter:

@moonssoulchild

@michaeltavon

Made in United States
North Haven, CT
10 December 2021